# SAINTS
# SHRINES
# & PILGRIMS

Keith Sugden

# CONTENTS

# PAGANS & PILGRIMS

Pilgrimage is by no means the sole domain of Christians. Think of the *Hadj* to Mecca, one of the five pillars of Islam; or consider those pagan supplicants at the Delphic Oracle or the great shrine to Aphrodite in Asia Minor. Naturally, ancient philosophy influenced the early Christians. Evangelists generally found it prudent to adapt the pagan beliefs to the new religion rather than simply destroy them, taking on board the old myths and sacred sites. A famous letter from Pope Gregory the Great to St Augustine instructs the 6th-century missionary to build his churches on ancient places of worship. Of course many Britons had been Christians under the Roman Empire, and at a few places in Britain, tradition or modern research claims that Christianity never died out during the pagan invasions of the Dark Ages – Glastonbury in Somerset and Deerhurst in Gloucestershire are among them.

St Augustine and his followers began their mission in England by converting the Saxon royal families; from that point the faith of the individual kings led to the replacement of the pagan beliefs. Some rulers became so devout that their own souls took precedence over the kingdom. Such was King Ina of Wessex, who abdicated, gave his throne to a kinsman and made the 'permanent pilgrimage' to Rome – where he spent the rest of his days. Many wealthy Englishmen of the day followed suit, trusting that by dying at Rome, close to the bearer of the keys of heaven, St Peter, they would stand the best possible chance on the Day of Judgement.

The temple of Stonehenge, a shrine of the moon and later of the sun, was a focus for prehistoric religion in Wessex for 1,700 years. Bronze Age chieftains sought to be buried within sight of it.

# PAGAN SITES

Two of Britain's most evocative and popular shrines are pagan in origin. The Isle of Avalon in Celtic mythology is the mystical land of the dead. For centuries, this paradise has been identified as a magical hill rising out of the Somerset Levels – Glastonbury Tor.

For the Romans and their British subjects, the hot springs of Aquae Sulis (modern Bath), unique in Britain, held an even greater attraction. A genuine little shrine-town developed there by the 3rd century AD, now beautifully excavated and explained in the Roman Baths Museum.

ABOVE: The Gorgon's head from the pediment of the temple in Bath, found in 1790 when the Pump Room was being built, also represents Sul, god of the sacred spring.

# MOTIVES & MEANS

In early Christian times only the wealthy could afford the pilgrimage to Rome and common Englishmen had to rest content with visiting a local shrine. Even then the choice of shrines must have been wide, with the memory of the foundation of their churches still fresh in the minds of the people, and the relics of hundreds of founders ('saints') close at hand, especially in Wales and Cornwall. By the time pilgrimage reached its heyday in the 14th century the phenomenon was enormous. During this period, the recorded numbers of pilgrims to Canterbury exceeded 200,000 a year, out of a total population in England estimated at just under four million on the outbreak of the Black Death in 1348.

The number of famous shrines grew and grew as monks and prelates vied to attract more pilgrims. Every single church was supposed to have a relic of some kind. Many judged the fame of towns, not on the size of the population or the quality of their products, but on the number and reputation of their relics. Some shrines had connections with numerous saints: 13 at Glastonbury. Other monasteries and churches possessed more relics than they knew what to do with – over 400 were said to exist at Canterbury, where 250 miracles were described in the six years after St Thomas's death.

The pilgrim, who had a home to return to, was distinct from the palmer, who had none. He was a professional pilgrim, living on nothing but alms and perpetually journeying from shrine to shrine. Men knew him by the palm or branch brought back from the Holy Land itself. Of course, being a palmer was a convenient cover for all kinds of escaped villeins, criminals, and those who found a settled existence or their fellow men too much to bear. Some palmers were known to have been adept at putting the evil eye on those common souls who shunned them.

ABOVE LEFT: A 12th-century style image of St Thomas Becket which is, in fact, one of Samuel Caldwell's 'deceptive recreations' of 1919 using medieval glass.

ABOVE RIGHT: The King's headstrong knights murder Archbishop Becket as he prays at a side altar in Canterbury Cathedral on 29 December 1170, shown in an almost contemporary psalter.

LEFT & RIGHT: A group of monks (left) and crusaders on horseback, from the 14th-century *Chronicle of St Denis*.

If a man was too sick, or busy, or lazy to go on pilgrimage for himself, it was common to employ a proxy to do the journey on his behalf, and the Church prudently recognised this as just as effective as making the journey himself. More commonly the proxy pilgrimage took place after death to gain some favour on the Day of Judgement; funds would be specified by will for the purpose.

People had many different motives for going on a pilgrimage. Mostly they went for religious reasons, but often the dominant factor was more secular. The most common motive was to pray at the shrine, appealing directly to the saint for success in a venture, which might be business, love, war or an attempt to throw off an illness or disability. Vows made at home, in a church or even in the heat of battle often obliged the believer to make long journeys as a thanksgiving for safe deliverance.

The obligatory gifts to the shrine gave the Church a truly vast income, and such was the prestige and wealth conferred on a church by the major miracle-working relics that theft of relics and fraud by monks were widespread in the Middle Ages.

# THE CELTIC SAINTS
## COLUMBA † CUTHBERT

The Celtic Church was a bastion of learning and artistic endeavour in a barbarous Europe and its contacts were international. The early monks moved at will around the seaways of western Britain – Dumnonia (the Cornish peninsula), Wales and Dalriada (the west of Scotland) – Ireland and Brittany, exploiting their common language. In those times any learned man who successfully founded a new church was likely to be canonised after a decent interval by his congregation – St Carantoc in Cornwall is an example. Such was the independence of each community under the Celtic rule. Energetic monks like Patrick, Columba, David or Piran were held in such esteem by their brethren and spiritual children that their churches soon became shrines to their memory and pilgrims braved every hardship to gain wisdom, guidance, comfort or healing from their physical remains. Among these inspiring figures, some are remembered for their extraordinary spirituality and some for the strangeness of their legends.

BELOW: Lindisfarne Priory, the site of a most important early centre of Christianity in the north, remains an evocative ruin and a goal for modern pilgrims.

## BRENDAN'S VOYAGE

There are many legends about St Patrick and his conversion of Ireland in the 5th century (see page 29). As a youth, he was enslaved by raiders in Ireland but he escaped, and spent many years in France. Patrick, impelled by recurrent dreams, was over 60 when he began his mission to Ireland. Later, an Irish monk called Brendan (c.486–575) made a voyage by coracle (a light boat covered in skins), perhaps even reaching North America. *The Voyage of St Brendan* enjoyed great popularity in the Middle Ages. It is a curious allegory of discovery combined with mysticism, sometimes describing nature in minute detail.

ABOVE: St John, seen in the *Lindisfarne Gospels* (c. AD 698), the most precious work of art to survive from early Christian England.

**Columba** is famous as the monk who evangelised Scotland, but this happened almost by accident. He was an Irish prince, born about 521, who became a follower of St Patrick. His character might be considered unsaintly: his actions show that he was forceful, stubborn and ambitious. In about 563 Columba's refusal to give up a manuscript, the Vulgate Gospels, culminated in vast bloodshed at the Battle of Cul Dremne. Regretting his stubbornness, he vowed to leave Ireland and never return. Columba sailed to Iona and was soon taking the word across the sea to the pagans of Mull and beyond into Argyll. There he converted the ruling house of Dalriada and then carried his mission all over Scotland. Following his death on Iona in 597, pilgrims came to venerate his relics in the church there.

**Cuthbert** was a shepherd boy from the Lammermuir Hills in the Scottish Lowlands. In 651, at the age of about 16, he entered the Celtic monastery of Melrose. Later in life he was prior of Lindisfarne (Holy Island) but wherever he served he was to go on long missionary journeys, preaching in remote villages and farmsteads in the hills. Returning to Lindisfarne, he would retire to the solitude of a hermitage on the bare slab of rock in the sea near the priory which still bears the name St Cuthbert's Isle. In 676, as a result of his 'long and spotless active life', he was allowed by his abbot and monks the special privilege of retiring to 'the stillness of divine contemplation' on one of the Farne Islands off the Northumbrian coast. In about 698, eleven years after his death and burial at Lindisfarne, the monks elevated his body to a new shrine and discovered its incorruption: the body had not decayed and the saint appeared as if asleep. From that time onward, it was an object of special veneration. The body, its shrine and the famous Lindisfarne Gospels began a long journey to a new home when the Vikings threatened Lindisfarne in 875. Only in 995 did they find a permanent home at Durham, where a Saxon church was specially built for them and consecrated three years later.

# THE CELTIC SAINTS
## DAVID (*DEWI SANT*) † WINEFREDE

St Michael's Mount, a mystical island off the coast of Cornwall, was the scene of two visions of the Archangel Michael and site of a Benedictine monastery.

**D**avid, or *Dewi Sant* in Welsh, is the patron saint of Wales who gave his name to the peninsula, Dewisland, containing his shrine, cathedral and city. The historical David is difficult to pin down because we are unsure how much written about his life by later chroniclers is distortion or sheer invention. As with the life of St Patrick, there is an almost complete lack of contemporary witness. We know for certain that David was a native Welshman who lived in the 6th century, and a great missionary and founder of monasteries in his country. He is said to have come from a royal line. According to legend, his mother was St Non, a nun at Ty Gwyn near Whitesands Bay, Pembrokeshire, who was seduced by Prince Sant and then spent the rest of her life in prayer and self-mortification. However, it is possible that she became a nun in widowhood after David's birth.

At David's baptism a fountain of the purest water burst forth spontaneously for the rite (this is now St Non's Well, a mile from St Davids Cathedral), while a blind monk holding the infant received his sight. After founding monasteries all over the land, David chose Vallis Rosina for his main community, which grew into the influential monastery and diocese of St Davids. David died and was buried in his own monastery. It is believed that his relics still exist in an ancient oak and iron casket which is now displayed in a stone niche behind the high altar – the very place, in fact, where the clergy hid them in the 16th century. A beautiful wrought-iron screen thwarts latter-day relic thieves. To see this shrine resplendent with daffodils, pilgrims should visit the cathedral on St David's Day (1 March).

In the 7th century, according to the myth, a young Welsh prince called Caradoc tried to seduce the virgin **Winefrede**. Failing in his objective but still inflamed with lust, he cut off her head 'which falling to the earth, deserved of God to

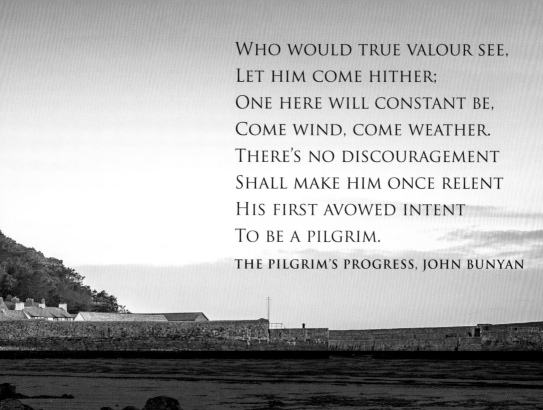

have a fountain of water to spring in the place, which to this day continueth'. Her tutor, Beuno, came out of the nearby church and discovering the calamity, cursed Caradoc so that the ground swallowed him up. Then taking Winefrede's head into Mass and calling on his people for their prayers, Beuno joined the head back with the body. Not only did Winefrede miraculously survive but she lived on for another 15 years.

This legend was only written down by an unknown monk in the 12th century. Six centuries later, in the Age of Reason, Dr William Fleetwood, Bishop of St Asaph, loathed this pilgrimage in his diocese and condemned it, declaring that he could not believe a story recorded 500 years after the subject's death. On the other hand, Winefrede seems very much like a pagan legend in a Christian dress. The story of a severed head miraculously rejoined to a body which springs back to life is typical of the often dark Celtic imagination and occurs several times in Celtic mythology.

LEFT: The peace and simplicity of St Non's Chapel, restored in the local early Christian style, evokes the spirit of St David, born at this place on the Pembrokeshire coast in the 6th century.

# THE PILGRIM ROUTES
## CANTERBURY † ROME † JERUSALEM † SANTIAGO

T he greatest pilgrimage in medieval times was to Jerusalem. After the Muslim conquest of Palestine in the 7th century, genuine pilgrims continued to travel to the Holy Sepulchre, the traditional site of Christ's burial. But the journey was difficult and dangerous, not to say expensive. During the Crusades, the few pilgrims who ventured on the journey needed the Knights Hospitaller to succour them and the Knights Templar to defend them.

Many pilgrims preferred a safer and cheaper option. For those willing to travel beyond their own country the most popular destinations were to the seven pilgrimage churches of Rome and the shrine of the apostle, St James the Greater, at Santiago de Compostela in Galicia (north-west Spain). Sometimes the Pope decreed, in a Papal Bull, the relative value of shrines to the pilgrim's soul; for example, Pope Calixtus II granted that two pilgrimages to St Davids in Pembrokeshire were equal to one pilgrimage to Rome; or in Latin, *Roma semel quantum, Dat bis Menevia tantum.*

The main roads to major medieval shrines achieved quite a high degree of organisation, with pilgrims forming convoys to travel from one hospice or inn to another.

The best-known account of life on the road and a specific pilgrimage is the *Codex Calixtenus*, edited by Aymery Picaud in about 1150. In five books he describes three routes from France which all combine at the Pyrenees to conduct the faithful to the shrine of St James of Compostela. This hallowed route across northern Spain to Santiago offers the modern traveller, whether as a pilgrim or as an historian, the most satisfying experience of any of the old pilgrimages.

Less well-known than Picaud's work is the itinerary of Sigeric, an Anglo-Saxon Archbishop of Canterbury who went on a pilgrimage to Rome in 990 to collect his pallium (mantle of office) from Pope John XV. A clerk or cleric in his retinue recorded all 80 stages of their journey, so it is possible to trace the exact route the 10th-century pilgrim followed from England to Rome. Following Sigeric's route today leads to the discovery

## THE PILGRIMS' WAY

The most popular pilgrimage during the Middle Ages was along the Pilgrims' Way from Winchester to Canterbury, to the shrine of England's most famous saint and martyr, St Thomas Becket. The archbishop's brutal and shocking murder, after his quarrel with King Henry II, led to his canonisation on Ash Wednesday in 1173. The largest number of medieval miracles in Britain occurred in the name of St Thomas.

Geoffrey Chaucer's *Canterbury Tales*, composed in about 1390, describes with wry humour the journey of a group of worldly pilgrims from London to Canterbury. Chaucer reveals a lack of esteem for the monastic life and the cult of relics, an increasingly common attitude in his day.

The Camino di Santiago (also known as The Way of St James) is one of the most popular pilgrim routes of today. This picture was taken near Astorga, Spain.

of numerous relics of the roads and their medieval traffic in the form of wayside crosses, especially elaborate wayside shrines, old street names and accommodation built for the faithful by religious orders or town guilds.

BELOW: Medieval pilgrims in front of the Holy Sepulchre in Jerusalem, from the *Book of Marvels*, on the travels of Marco Polo. They wear traditional costume and one of them makes a donation to the shrine.

ABOVE: A medieval map of Christendom showing Jerusalem at the centre of the world. Pilgrims to the Holy Land faced many dangers and were protected on the journey by the knights of the Crusades.

# THE PILGRIM'S JOURNEY

T he first stage in the medieval pilgrim's journey was usually the ceremony of leaving his home parish. After Mass and special prayers, the priest consecrated the pilgrim's scrip (a wallet similar to a modern fishing bag) and bourdon (his tall staff), sprinkling each with holy water. Then his friends and relatives led him out of the village with the cross borne high before them and gave him their blessing at the parish boundary. He would also carry a letter from his priest or his temporal lord to act as a recommendation of his genuine status to the pious and charitable.

How would he be recognised on the road? To wear the pilgrim's costume was both an honour and a penance, which served to identify him and help in begging for alms along the way. He wore a long and coarse woollen robe, brown or russet in colour and big enough to wrap around him for sleeping. A cross decorated the sleeve. His large round hat had a broad brim, usually turned up at the front to display his pilgrim badges – the symbolic shell and leaden images from the shrines he had already visited. Slung on lanyards around his neck he carried a scrip, a large knife, a flask for water and a rosary. The scrip was for spare pairs of hosen (stockings), two day's food and essential ointment for the feet. Finally, he carried a long stout staff, used for vaulting over streams, climbing hills and as defence against outlaws. It might be tipped with a hollow metal ball, the jangling 'Canterbury bell'.

## PILGRIM CROSSES

Wayside crosses served as waymarks to reassure travellers that they were on the right road and as roadside shrines, where they could offer prayers for a safe journey. Old maps and records indicate where some of them once stood. They were often situated where they could be seen from a great distance, at old crossroads on a pilgrim route. Most of these have disappeared but two fine examples survive on the route to the shrine of Our Lady at Walsingham: Binham Cross on the road from the miraculous Holy Rood of Bromholme, and Hockley cum Wilton Cross on the road from Ely.

Pilgrimage was largely a summer occupation and presumably people often slept under hedges or in barns. The accommodation which survives in England from the heyday of pilgrimage varies from hospices run by monks or a dedicated charity, to monasteries whose rules obliged the brethren to offer hospitality to any traveller, and common inns. The Hospital of Newark at Maidstone was a fine example of a hospice supported by a charity. Archbishop Boniface built it in 1261 to receive pilgrims to Canterbury, although it is several miles from the Pilgrims' Way. Now only its Early English chapel survives and is in use as the chancel of St Peter's church.

Canterbury had many hospices, such as the Hospital of St Thomas the Martyr, now known as the King's Bridge Hospital and founded, according to its charter, by the 'glorious St Thomas the Martyr to receive poor wayfaring men'. The Norman crypt and

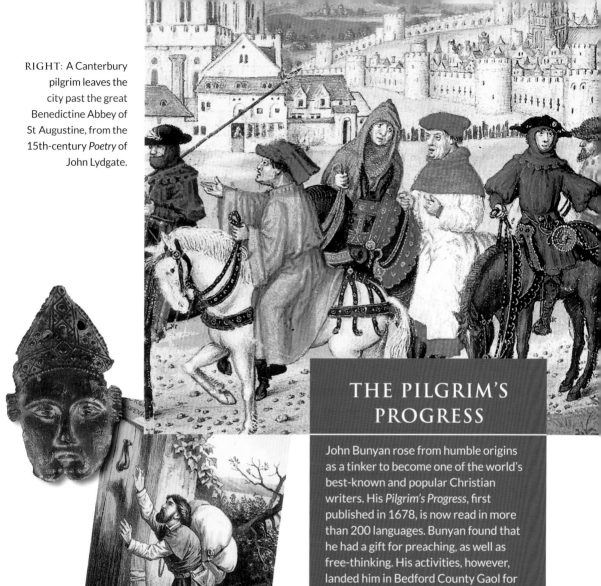

## THE PILGRIM'S PROGRESS

John Bunyan rose from humble origins as a tinker to become one of the world's best-known and popular Christian writers. His *Pilgrim's Progress*, first published in 1678, is now read in more than 200 languages. Bunyan found that he had a gift for preaching, as well as free-thinking. His activities, however, landed him in Bedford County Gaol for 12 years. There he 'dreamed a dream' and wrote his famous book about a pilgrimage through the Slough of Despond, Vanity Fair, the Hill of Difficulty and onwards to the Celestial City.

later refectory and chapel can still be seen. Other pilgrims lodged in the great priory of Christ Church (the cathedral), where a 15th-century extension known as Chillenden Chambers survives as part of the Archdeacon of Canterbury's house. Smaller numbers dispersed to the Hospital of St John in Northgate, the great Augustinian abbey or guest houses run by the mendicant friars.

ABOVE FAR LEFT: A leaden pilgrim badge in the form of the head of St Thomas Becket, of the type sold to visitors as tokens of their pilgrimage to Canterbury. The badge (on view in the Canterbury Heritage Museum ©) was a vital part of the medieval pilgrim's costume.

ABOVE LEFT: A pilgrim travels with the customary scrip (pouch) and staff, in an illustration from John Bunyan's famous tale.

15

# WALKING THE PILGRIM WAYS

**M**odern pilgrims often travel by car or coach to a popular shrine such as St Thomas at Canterbury or Our Lady at Walsingham, yet there are many who still prefer to go on foot. They are to be seen, especially, on the Way of St James in the north of Spain. In Britain, our inspiration comes from the writer Hilaire Belloc, who wore the three mantles of faithful pilgrim, observant local historian and incorrigible trespasser. He trudged from Alsace to the Vatican and left us a witty account in *The Path to Rome* (1902). Then he muddied his boots on our own Pilgrims' Way from Winchester to Canterbury, describing what remained to be seen from medieval times and merrily theorising in *The Old Road* (1904). Since then there have been several other guidebooks to The Pilgrims' Way and plenty of authors have written about miracles, relics and the architecture of pilgrimage.

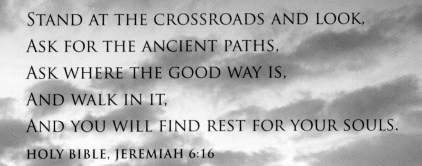

STAND AT THE CROSSROADS AND LOOK,
ASK FOR THE ANCIENT PATHS,
ASK WHERE THE GOOD WAY IS,
AND WALK IN IT,
AND YOU WILL FIND REST FOR YOUR SOULS.

HOLY BIBLE, JEREMIAH 6:16

## PILGRIM ROUTES

Old Sarum to Glastonbury
Cirencester to Bath
Oban to Iona
Hexham to Lindisfarne
St Piran's Cell to St Michael's Mount
Llanfihangel Abercowin to St Davids Cathedral
Winchester to Canterbury
Beverley Minster to York Minster
St Asaph to St Winefrede's, Holywell
Ely to Walsingham

The causeway leading to the
Holy Island of Lindisfarne, is still
a well-trodden path for pilgrims.
Centuries ago these pilgrims would
have followed the natural sand and
mud flats.

# SAINTS & SHRINES
## BEVERLEY † CANTERBURY † CHESTER

Medieval beliefs about relics are central to pilgrimage. Relics inspired the medieval faithful with a sense of power and mystery. The power suffused the physical remains that a holy person left behind on earth, and the supplicants could, by adoring the relics, gain the intercession of the saint in their lives. In this way the saints were simultaneously present in heaven and in their earthly relics. If a saint's relics were divided and dispersed to other churches, their power was not diminished; a finger bone was as precious as a whole body.

A relic was kept for its own security, and for its greater glory, in a shrine, a term which refers specifically to its receptacle (*scrinium*). More generally, the term means the shrine-base with its elaborate superstructure and cover which surround the small jewelled reliquary. More widely, shrine refers to a holy place, such as Canterbury Cathedral.

England has some big parish churches but none is quite as huge as **Beverley Minster**. And at Beverley it is not just the size which impresses, for here there is a standard of design, masonry and sculpture far higher than at many of England's medieval cathedrals.

**John of Beverley** had the honour of ordaining the Venerable Bede, famous chronicler of early Christian times. Later he became Bishop of York. Among his many cures was that of a deaf and dumb boy: so famous is this miracle that he is remembered today as the patron saint of the deaf and dumb. Following his death in 721, St John's relics rested in a magnificent shrine in the ambulatory behind the high altar at Beverley, the most usual place in a large medieval church. Pilgrims would have approached along the choir aisles. The relics were moved to the nave after the shrine's destruction at the Reformation.

Pilgrims to the medieval shrine of **St Thomas Becket** in **Canterbury Cathedral** found themselves well organised. Monks met them, marshalled them into orderly groups and conducted them into the cathedral through the very same door in the north transept used by both Becket and his attackers on 29 December 1170. The first station was the spot where Thomas was brutally cut down, the whole scene no doubt vividly described by the practised guide, as the pilgrims knelt on the cold flags and looked in horror on the tip of de Brito's sword, shattered by the mighty blow that had split the martyr's skull in two.

The second station was the high altar where the body lay throughout the fatal night. Finally the pilgrims descended to the Norman crypt and prayed at the miraculous tomb itself. On 7 July 1220 the relics were translated (moved) to their new shrine above the high altar in the new Gothic cathedral. As it was the most famous shrine in the kingdom, Henry VIII's commissioners took special care to destroy everything at the Dissolution.

The twin west towers and the great central tower ('Bell Harry') still rise above the city of Canterbury to welcome pilgrims to Britain's most famous shrine.

RIGHT: A 14th-century bench-end in Chester Cathedral's splendid choir shows a pilgrim with his staff and characteristic hat.

ABOVE: Modern medallion showing St John of Beverley's cure of a dumb and diseased youth, as described by the Venerable Bede.

**St Werburgh**, whose shrine is found in the Lady Chapel in **Chester Cathedral**, was the daughter of Wulfere, the Saxon king of Mercia. She became a nun and, through her piety, an abbess noted for her reforms. After she died, in the early 8th century at her nunnery of Trentham, many miracles were reported from her tomb at Hanbury in Staffordshire. Her relics came to Chester to protect them from ravages by the Danes. The church was specially enlarged to house her relics. After the Norman Conquest it was rebuilt and converted to a Benedictine abbey. Werburgh's shrine remained a great centre of pilgrimage until the Reformation; part of its stone base survives in today's cathedral. Her main emblem in art is a goose, which, according to Goscelin's *Life*, she was supposed to have restored to life.

# SAINTS & SHRINES
## CHICHESTER † DURHAM † ELY

**R**ichard of Wych, bishop of **Chichester** 1245–53, was born at Droitwich in 1197, the son of a yeoman farmer. He studied in the universities of Oxford, Paris and Bologna. In 1235 he returned to Oxford to lecture in canon law and soon became chancellor. Following his ordination in 1242, he became priest in the Kent parishes of Charing and Deal. In 1244 he was elected bishop of Chichester, but Henry III and part of the chapter refused to accept him. After an appeal to the authority of Rome, Pope Innocent IV consecrated Richard bishop at Lyons. Besides being a model diocesan bishop, Richard enthusiastically preached the crusades, not as a political expedition, but as a means of making access to the Holy Land easier for pilgrims. He was canonised in 1262 and his relics were translated to a splendid new shrine behind the high altar in his cathedral in 1276. The shrine was despoiled by Henry VIII's commissioners in 1538, and Richard's body was reburied secretly. In art, he is depicted with a chalice at his feet, in memory of the occasion when he dropped the chalice at Mass, but the wine miraculously remained unspilt.

ABOVE: Cuthbert's precious garnet-and-gold Pectoral Cross, dating from the 7th century.

RIGHT: The tomb of St Cuthbert, the north of England's most popular saint, behind the high altar of Durham Cathedral, where he was reburied during the Reformation.

The cult and fame of **St Cuthbert** was responsible for the rebuilding of **Durham Cathedral** in the magnificent Norman style. In about 1140 an attempt by Bishop de Puiset to build a Lady Chapel at the east end failed due to subsidence – this was attributed to the displeasure of St Cuthbert, buried nearby. As a result, the bishop built at the west end of the Romanesque Galilee Chapel. In these surroundings, unique in England, the cult of St Cuthbert flourished. A huge catalogue of wealth accumulated but it was all surrendered to the crown in 1540, along with the monastery. Following the destruction of his shrine, St Cuthbert was reburied on the same spot beneath a plain marble slab.

The Venerable Bede describes the life of the saint who founded **Ely Cathedral**. Despite two noble marriages, **Etheldreda** remained a virgin and retreated to an island in the Fens which had been part of the dowry of her first marriage. There she founded a nunnery in 673 and died in 679. Sixteen years after Etheldreda's burial, her body was found free from decay – then seen as the surest sign of sanctity. In the 13th century the east end of the great cathedral was rebuilt to honour her tomb – before the Reformation her shrine was in the place of honour immediately in front of the high altar.

ABOVE: The choir at Ely Cathedral, rebuilt in honour of the founder, St Etheldreda, in the 13th century. Her shrine stood, rather unusually, in front of the high altar between the choir stalls.

Fragments from the base of the shrine can still be seen next to the tomb of Bishop Hugh de Northwold who extended the cathedral. The translation of her body to its new shrine is observed on 17 October, St Etheldreda's Fair, commonly called St Awdry's Fair. So cheap and showy was the finery, especially lace, sold there that the contraction of 'St Awdry' gives us the English word 'tawdry'. But there is nothing tawdry about the marvellous cathedral, with its famous 'Octagon' tower, which rises like a huge ship above the Fens and the little buildings of this well-preserved old market town.

# SAINTS & SHRINES
## HEREFORD † LICHFIELD † LINCOLN

**T**homas Cantelupe, known as St Thomas of **Hereford**, was born in 1218 at Hambledon in Buckinghamshire into a noble and powerful Norman family. His uncle, the bishop of Worcester, supervised his education and prepared Thomas for high office in both church and state. He went to study in Oxford, Paris and Orleans, returning, like St Richard of Chichester before him, to be chancellor at Oxford. Following the defeat of Henry III at the Battle of Lewes, Thomas became chancellor of England for a year until Simon de Montfort's defeat at the Battle of Evesham. He left the country and returned to Paris as lecturer in canon law. In 1275 the canons of Hereford elected him their bishop but Thomas soon quarrelled violently with John Pecham, Archbishop of Canterbury. He found himself excommunicated and resorted to the papal court at Orvieto in central Italy, but died on 25 August 1282 at Montefiascone. He was buried at Orvieto but his heart and bones were returned to Hereford Cathedral. How the shrine survived the Reformation is a mystery.

**Chad**, a much-loved monk, was brought out of retirement in his monastery to be Bishop of Mercia in 669. The Venerable Bede recounts, in his History of the English Church and People, written in 731, that Chad died of disease on 2 March 672, an event foretold by a choir of angels seven days earlier at **Lichfield**, where his cult has since remained. Bede says that he was first buried in St Mary's Church, then in St Peter's. At both shrines frequent miracles of healing attested to Chad's virtues. In 1148 the relics were translated to a shrine at the high altar of the Norman cathedral. The cult was so popular that in 1330, at a cost of £2000, Bishop Langton built another shrine, placed behind the high altar for easier access to pilgrims. The site is still marked today.

Such a fine cathedral also acquired other relics: the Sacrist's Roll for 1345 lists 'the relics of divers saints ... some of the bones of St Laurence, some of Golgotha ... part of the sepulchre of the Blessed Virgin Mary ... part of the finger and cowl of St William, some of the bones of St Stephen ...'. Episodes in Chad's life are shown in six panels of stained glass in the Chapter House and in a Victorian tiled floor by Minton in the presbytery.

ABOVE: St Chad preferred to make his missionary journeys around Mercia on foot. In this Victorian roundel at Lichfield Cathedral, Archbishop Theodore instructs him to ride a horse around his diocese.

**Hugh** was a strong-minded and zealous bishop at **Lincoln** who survived an argument with Henry II over the excommunication of a royal forester. Hugh was conspicuous by his unbounded charity, especially towards lepers, and his

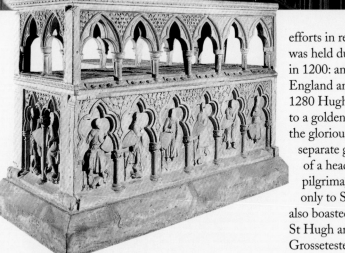

efforts in rebuilding the cathedral. His funeral was held during a council of state at Lincoln in 1200: among the bearers were King John of England and King William of Scotland. In 1280 Hugh's body was translated in splendour to a golden shrine in the place of honour in the glorious Angel Choir. The head graced a separate golden chef (reliquary in the shape of a head) nearby. The scale of the pilgrimage to his shrine was then second only to St Thomas at Canterbury. Lincoln also boasted three other shrines, those of Little St Hugh and two more bishops, Robert Grosseteste and John of Dalderby.

ABOVE: Few medieval shrines escaped destruction by Henry VIII's commissioners, but Hereford's St Thomas Cantelupe's survived the destruction. Set on a pedestal of Purbeck marble, the niches at the base of the shrine contain statues of 14 Knights Templar.

23

# SAINTS & SHRINES
## RIPON † ST ALBAN'S † ST EDMUNDSBURY † SALISBURY

A new Anglican diocese was created in 1836 at an attractive market town in rural Yorkshire. Only then did **Ripon** Minster become a cathedral. Today it is a mixture of styles. It has a Saxon crypt and displays in its parts the development of the Romanesque and Gothic styles. The cathedral contains the shrine of **St Wilfrid**. He was the robust protagonist whose arguments defeated the Celtic partisans, or followers of St Columba, at the Synod of Whitby in 664. Elected Bishop of York, he converted the Northumbrian church to the Roman custom and introduced the Benedictine rule to northern monasteries. After an argument over the division of his see, he fell from power, appealed to the Pope (the first time an English bishop did this) and was finally restored to his monastery at Ripon, where he was buried in 709.

St Alban is honoured as Britain's first martyr (*c.*209), suffering his fate for sheltering a Christian priest fleeing the persecution of Septimus Severus. According to legend the executioner's eyes fell out as his sword struck off the head. Passionate debates arose about St Alban's bones. In the two centuries between the Norman Conquest and the account by the monk Matthew Paris so many lies had been told about the saint's relics that it became difficult for anyone to claim that they had the bones of the protomartyr if, indeed, they had ever been preserved. The elaborate and richly bejewelled shrine of *c.*1302–08 was destroyed in 1539 but two thousand fragments of its tall pedestal of Purbeck marble were discovered in 1872, built into a wall blocking off the east end of the church. Painstakingly reassembled then, and again in 1991, it still gives a hint of the richness of this most worldly of medieval abbeys, although its canopy was destroyed at the Reformation.

**Edmund**, a Saxon prince, inherited the throne of the East Angles at the age of 15, at a time when the incursions of the Danes were

BELOW: A detail of the modern window in the Pilgrim Chapel at Ripon Cathedral commemorates the cult of St Wilfrid, which flourished in the former minster. The crypt of Wilfrid's church is a rare survival.

increasing. According to tradition, the young Edmund fought the Danes in 869 at the battle of Thetford. Dismayed by the carnage of his people, he surrendered himself to the enemy in the hope that the sacrifice of his own life might save his subjects. After a severe beating, he was tied naked to a tree, scourged with whips, riddled with arrows and finally beheaded. A legend says that the discarded head was found by a wolf, who followed the funeral procession at Hoxne until the head was rejoined to the body. Thirty-three years later, following a series of miracles, the relics were translated to a shrine at Bury, where the cult of the last king of East Anglia flourished. Although the arms of the city of Bury St Edmunds incorporate a wolf's head to this day, the site of the shrine is now lost and little remains of the once gigantic abbey.

ABOVE: This detail from a hanging embroidered by Sybil Andrews in 1975 shows Edmund, king and martyr, shot by Danish bowmen during their invasion. Also depicted is the legendary wolf who guarded Edmund's head.

According to a 15th-century document, **Osmund**, bishop of Old Sarum 1078–99, was a nephew of William the Conqueror and came to England as chaplain with the Duke's army in 1066. This may well be true, as he was employed by the king in a civil capacity to prepare part of the Domesday Book. He was also present at the consecration of Battle Abbey. He perhaps even held the chancellorship before being conse- crated bishop of Old Sarum in 1078. He himself consecrated the new **Salisbury** cathedral on the hilltop in 1092 and was active in establishing a Norman chapter and hierarchy. Later, his *Use of Sarum*, a service book, met with almost universal acceptance in Britain and Ireland. Osmund was canonised in 1457.

RIGHT: This tomb is traditionally identified as part of the medieval shrine of St Osmund, whose body was moved from Old Sarum and reinterred at the new Salisbury Cathedral in 1226.

# SAINTS & SHRINES
## WESTMINSTER † WINCHESTER † WORCESTER † YORK

**W**estminster Abbey still venerates the shrine of King **Edward the Confessor**, builder of the late Saxon abbey. The well-documented reconstruction by Henry III further elevated the status of this royal shrine. In 1241 he ordered a new monument to be made of gold and marble. Both king and queen presented jewels or money for the extremely lavish work. This great shrine survives, stripped of valuables but surrounded by the tombs of most of England's medieval kings. Nearby in the abbey, the tomb of Henry VII was almost an official shrine. The tomb of this king, a usurper who defeated Richard III at the Battle of Bosworth, serves the purpose of legitimising his Tudor regime.

**Winchester** became the focus for trade and travellers through Southampton, and by late Saxon times the city was the capital of England. The Normans, too, favoured Winchester, which continued to be the land's royal and administrative

LEFT: Winchester Cathedral marks the starting point of the Pilgrim's Way to Canterbury.

centre until about 1250. This is reflected in the magnificence of Winchester Cathedral, which was the longest and finest church in Norman England.

Quite apart from its strategic and political importance, the 12th-century city had famous 'workshops' of carving and manuscript illumination. The Winchester School was one of the great triumphs of English artistic genius. It was also esteemed for the shrine of **St Swithun**, its 9th-century bishop during the period of the great monastic reforms under St Dunstan. This pilgrimage site was highly popular long before the murder of Thomas Becket in 1170. Only a few fragments remain of the medieval shrine but the cathedral continues to be the starting point for the Pilgrims' Way to Canterbury.

As an esteemed novice, **Wulfstan** was admitted as a monk to **Worcester** cathedral-monastery before the Norman Conquest. Rising to be prior under the bishop, he travelled about baptising the children of the poor because, it is said, the secular clergy refused to do this without a fee. Wulfstan made himself useful to King Harold but then swiftly made submission to William the Conqueror at Berkhampstead. In 1088, he denounced English and Welsh rebels marching on Worcester, thereby, according to tradition, securing their defeat. He was buried at Worcester and immediately regarded as a saint, although he was not formally canonised until 1203. King John on his deathbed commended his soul to God and St Wulfstan and was buried next to the shrine.

**William Fitzherbert** was of noble birth, the son of Herbert, Henry I's treasurer, and had a luxurious upbringing, probably at the Norman royal court in Winchester. When the Archbishop of **York**, Thurstan, died in 1140, a furious and prolonged dispute arose about the succession, involving King Stephen, the Cistercians at Fountains Abbey, the Archbishop of Canterbury, the great St Bernard of Clairvaux and Pope Innocent II. When William finally became archbishop, tragedy struck within a month. He was seized with a sudden illness while celebrating Mass in his own minster. Poisoning was suspected and antidotes were administered at once but to no avail. William died eight days later, with Archdeacon Osbert accused of poisoning the eucharistic chalice. William was admitted to the calendar of saints in 1227.

ABOVE: Wulfstan offering his church. Parts of Wulfstan's cathedral at Worcester, built in the Romanesque style, still survive, and include the largest Norman crypt in England.

RIGHT: St William of York, a minor figure promoted in life beyond his abilities and in death beyond his miracles, from the Bolton Hours, c.1420, in York Minster Library.

# SURVIVAL AND REVIVAL

Holywell in North Wales is a shrine where the adherents of the old faith never let go. During the Middle Ages this ancient pagan well became one of the most popular Christian places of pilgrimage due to the legend of St Winefrede. During the Reformation, for reasons which remain obscure, it also became a focus of activity by Catholic recusants (nonconformists). Pilgrims never stopped coming to the shrine, despite the best efforts of the Anglican bishop and the civil authorities. Today the shrine is still visited by thousands of pilgrims every year; not too many to destroy the peace of this most ornamental of Gothic chapels, but enough to keep the candles burning constantly.

At Walsingham, during the 20th century, both Anglicans and Catholics have revived the pilgrimage of medieval kings, each maintaining a separate shrine, but neither on the original sacred site. The pilgrimages at Glastonbury, begun in 1924 as a small celebration of faith, now involve some 3,000 people (Catholics, Anglicans and Orthodox Christians), meant travelling from far afield to take part. Canterbury, too, has benefited from this modern enthusiasm for an old custom. A greater number of genuine pilgrims now arrive at the shrine of St Thomas Becket than at any time since 1500.

St Patrick's Island in Lough Derg, County Donegal, is the scene of the most rigorous pilgrimage in Britain or Ireland, where devotees assemble for a strict three-day penance on the saint's day.

# OUR LADY AT LOURDES

A picturesque French town nestling at the foot of the Pyrenees receives five million visitors a year. They come here because of the most famous vision of modern times. On 11 February 1858, a poor girl aged 14 years, Bernadette Soubirous, met and later spoke with the Virgin Mary in a cave called Massabielle. The vision said, among other things, 'I am the Immaculate Conception' and 'I do not promise to make you happy in this world but the other'. The story spread like wildfire, Bernadette was canonised in 1933, crutches now hang at the grotto and the little town hosts the most impressive Marian cult in Europe.

RIGHT: 20th-century piety at Lourdes: A statue of St Bernadette in front of an apse mosaic showing the schoolgirl's famous vision of the Virgin Mary.

In the far west of Ireland, there are three shrines with an even stronger hold on their devotees. Nowhere else in the British Isles is pilgrimage taken more seriously than at Lough Derg in county Donegal, where pilgrims assemble on St Patrick's Island on the saint's day for an extremely rigorous three-day penance to commemorate his fast. Croagh Patrick is a mountain of rock and scree on the Atlantic coast of county Mayo, where St Patrick meditated for 40 days and prayed that Ireland should remain forever Christian. On the last Sunday in July, 'Reek Sunday' as it is known, some 60,000 Roman Catholics commemorate Patrick's devotion. It has been described as 'an extraordinary, almost medieval sight. Above you, the line stretches along the brow of Ireland's Holy Mountain till it disappears in the thickening cloud. Below you, hundreds more are on their way up or down.

At Knock, also in County Mayo, pilgrims visit the site of a vision that was witnessed by the entire village in 1879. St Joseph, the Blessed Virgin Mary and the *Agnus Dei* appeared over the gable of the modest church. In 1979 the villagers persuaded Pope Paul to bless the site on its centenary. On that occasion no fewer than one million Irish men and women, nearly one third of the population of the Republic of Ireland, converged on Knock. Such is the continuing power of miracles, holy places and the spirit of pilgrimage.

It is this enduring spirit which inspires people today, as of old, to set out to walk the ancient ways, visit the holy places and explore the roots of their faith. Whatever the motive for setting out, whatever the hardships encountered along the way, the pilgrim's reward is the secret joy of spiritual discovery.

# SAINTS & SHRINES

ATLANTIC

OCEAN

SCOTLAND

NORTH

SEA

Iona

NORTHERN
IRELAND

Lough Derg

Knock
Croagh Patrick

EIRE

IRISH SEA

Lindisfarne

Durham

Ripon

York

Beverley

ENGLAND

Holywell

Chester

Lincoln

Bromholme

Ilam

Walsingham

Lichfield

WALES

Worcester

Ely

St Edmundsbury

Hereford

Hailes

St Davids

St Alban's

Llandaff

Dorchester

Waltham Abbey

Westminster

Glastonbury

Salisbury

Canterbury

Winchester

Whitchurch

Chichester

ENGLISH CHANNEL

St Michael's
Mount

BEVERLEY MINSTER  St John of Beverley

BROMHOLME, NORFOLK  The Holy Rood

CANTERBURY CATHEDRAL  St Thomas Becket

CHESTER CATHEDRAL  St Werburgh

CHICHESTER CATHEDRAL  St Richard

CROAGH PATRICK, COUNTY MAYO  St Patrick

DORCHESTER ABBEY, OXFORDSHIRE  St Birinus

DURHAM CATHEDRAL  St Cuthbert

ELY CATHEDRAL  St Etheldreda

GLASTONBURY ABBEY  St Dunstan

HAILES ABBEY, GLOUCESTERSHIRE  The Holy Blood

HEREFORD CATHEDRAL  St Thomas Cantelupe

HOLYWELL, FLINTSHIRE  St Winefrede

ILAM, STAFFORDSHIRE  St Bertelin

IONA ABBEY  St Columba

KNOCK, COUNTY MAYO  St Joseph, Virgin Mary, Agnus Dei

LICHFIELD CATHEDRAL  St Chad (and holy well)

LINCOLN CATHEDRAL  St Hugh and Little St Hugh

LINDISFARNE PRIORY  St Cuthbert, Oswald, Aidan

LLANDAFF CATHEDRAL  St Teilo

LOUGH DERG, COUNTY DONEGAL  St Patrick

RIPON CATHEDRAL  St Wilfrid

SALISBURY CATHEDRAL  St Osmund

ST ALBAN'S CATHEDRAL  St Alban

ST DAVID'S CATHEDRAL  St David (Dewis)

ST EDMUNDSBURY CATHEDRAL  St Edmund

ST MICHAEL'S MOUNT  Archangel Michael

WALSINGHAM, NORFOLK  Our Lady

WALTHAM ABBEY, HERTS  The Miraculous Cross

WESTMINSTER ABBEY  Edward the Confessor

WINCHESTER CATHEDRAL  St Swithun

WHITCHURCH CANONICORUM, DORSET  St Candida or Wita

WORCESTER CATHEDRAL  St Wulfstan

YORK MINSTER  St William of York

Most of the saints and shrines on the map are
mentioned in this guidebook; however space
does not permit a comprehensive list.

PILGRIMS' WA

WINCHESTER - CANTERBU

A. D. 2000